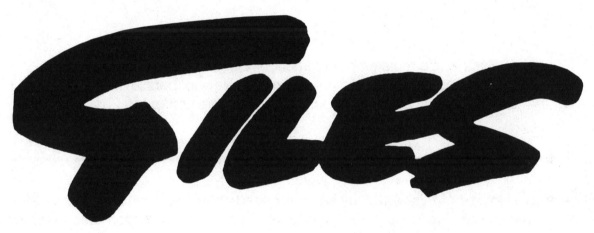

The Collection 2014

An Hachette UK Company
www.hachette.co.uk

First published in Great Britain in 2013 by Hamlyn,
a division of Octopus Publishing Group Ltd, Endeavour House, 189 Shaftesbury Avenue,
London, WC2H 8JY

www.octopusbooks.co.uk

Cartoons supplied by British Archive
Cartoons compiled by John Field

ISBN: 978-0-600-62456-1

A CIP catalogue record for this book is available
from the British Library.

Printed and bound in China

1 2 3 4 5 6 7 8 9 10

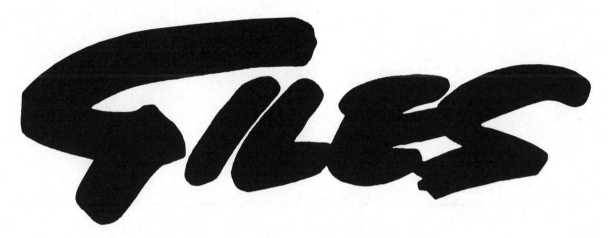

The Collection 2014

compiled by John Field

EXPRESS NEWSPAPERS

hamlyn

Contents

Foreword

John Sergeant

When the best comedians make an appearance they are greeted with smiles, and sometimes even laughter. You expect them to cheer you up and they do. And so it is with Giles, or to be more accurate GILES. He was not only a brilliant draughtsman, carefully setting the scene with meticulous detail and lovable characters; he was also able to draw you instantly into a world of his own.

All his cartoons have a familiar look. It is a style which he created and repeated for over fifty years. Sometimes in the annuals there would be a splash of colour, but in his usual newspaper work it was the sharp contrast of black and white, which allowed him to make his point and emphasise the joke. Some cartoonists get a laugh by being cruel, even savage, but that was not his way. Giles was not out to shock or cast blame, he wanted to charm us into accepting that we can, all of us, be pretty daft. That is not to say that ridiculous behaviour is spread equally around the country or across every class. He had his favourites.

Laughing at authority is a staple source of Giles humour. At school there are subjects aplenty. Teachers are usually funny, particularly when trying to be taken seriously. They can be given nicknames, like Chalkie and it helps if their heads resemble human skulls. Small kids are funny if they are squat and are fearlessly prepared to fight boys much bigger than themselves.

Army officers are also fairly risible, and the more posh the better. If you want to be certain of raising a laugh you should look no further than the Household Cavalry. Who better to intervene in a strike or any kind of civil disturbance than breast plated men who may trip over their spurs? When it comes to businessmen, their uniform of suits and bowler hats achieves the same effect.

In the countryside, Giles is clearly on the side of decent men of toil, farmers working in the blinding rain, looking askance at the gentry, who can't wait to down another gin and tonic.

As for animals there are plenty of pigs and cows we can sympathise with, putting up with supposedly superior farm hands. And there are foxes running rings around all of us.

To me, the funniest of all the characters created by Giles is the grandma. Her age has made her impervious to criticism, or more likely she was always that way inclined. Her hat is worn, rammed down upon her head as if to say, I don't care. She can do what she wants, even if this invariably makes her absurd.

With Giles you can always see something in these marvellous drawings which is bound to amuse. They are best appreciated as works of art, timelessly funny examples of British humour at its best.

Introduction: Giles and Society

For half a century, there were few aspects of British life on which Giles did not comment through his cartoons. At the height of his work, he was producing three, and sometimes four, a week, applying his unique sense of humour and his fascination with the intricacies and eccentricities of British life. He also had the inherent ability to see and illustrate events from the point-of-view of the man in the street.

With so many possible stories and issues to comment on, Giles was, on some occasions, uncertain as to which aspect of the day's news to illustrate. This dilemma is displayed in the cartoon of him at work in the studio at his farm near Ipswich, which appeared on February 3, 1950, (see Journalism). It shows Joan, his wife, being the good housewife, attempting to clean up his studio. It is recorded, however, that in reality, she actually played a more important role in his work: going through the newspapers first thing in the morning, underlining any stories which could form the subject of that day's cartoon. In the cartoon shown, the choice is obviously between the rather important, and frightening, news that the world was increasingly able to blow itself up, with the US experimenting with hydrogen bombs, and, perhaps of less international importance, the rising cost of animal food, with the UK government concerned about its impact on food production – summed up by Giles, as pigeon food.

This year, the choice of themes covers a range of subjects in which Giles seemed to have a particular interest, although it has to be accepted that there were very few areas of British life which Giles did not find interesting or use as a basis for a cartoon.

Police

Giles generally had a very good relationship throughout his life with the local police forces in Suffolk, being invited to many of their social events and frequently being asked to produce designs for the covers of the menus for their dinners. He usually portrayed the police in a good light, sometimes illustrating, in his way, the difficulties they encountered trying to enforce the law (see July 11, 1963). Occasionally, however, some event would persuade him to use his power as a cartoonist to get his revenge, in a relatively gentle way, following some annoyance. After an appearance in court on a speeding offence, Giles produced a cartoon showing a policeman, resembling the one who had given evidence against him, on traffic duty. Nearby, looking rather pleased, was a small dog, having just relieved itself against the policeman's leg.

Sport

As you would expect, working in a country which had developed many of the world's most popular sports, Giles would use this as a basis for a large number of his cartoons. Of course, football featured strongly but he managed to cover almost the whole range of British sports. As a young man he, himself, participated in horse and motor racing and, later, was an avid sailor, keeping his own yacht on the nearby River Deben. These all feature in his cartoons but his repertoire covered just about all of our other sporting activities. In one cartoon (July 5, 1962), he contrived to combine the Henley Regatta, Wimbledon and the test match between England and Pakistan – all sports which, for many people, lie at the heart of British summer sporting life.

Journalism

Giles spent almost his entire career working in the newspaper industry. It could be said, then, that this chapter has him working on home ground with an insider knowledge of the hectic life of many correspondents (see October 22, 1968). Giles did not, however, hold back with his sometimes incisive sense of humour when confronted with issues on his own turf. He did not hesitate to include his own boss, Lord Beaverbrook, as the butt of the humour (see March 22, 1962). He was also able to feed a supposed feud with his fellow *Express* journalist, Jean Rook – (cartoons dated June 19, 1973 and November 18, 1986).

The Economy

With many economic ups and downs facing our country during the period of his drawing life, Giles had plenty of material for his cartoons on this subject. This chapter touches upon a wide range of issues affecting our economy including rationing and the long period of austerity which followed the Second World War (September 21, 1949), various shortages relating to fuel and other resources (March 5, 1957), the devaluation of the pound and other economic setbacks which confronted our country. It is obvious from these cartoons that Giles usually had sympathy with the plight of the ordinary person facing a succession of difficulties (see April 6, 1951).

Shopping

So far as I am aware, there is no great evidence that Giles himself was a committed shopper. There is little doubt, however, that, with his obvious pleasure in drawing crowd scenes, he was attracted by the opportunity, particularly during the pre-Christmas period, to capture the melée created by frenzied shopping activity (December 21, 1954). In consequence, many of his "shopping" cartoons appeared during the lead-up to Christmas. It is also generally recognised that much of the pleasure to be gained from studying his cartoons is not simply the actual point of humour contained but also the wealth of background detail he frequently included. This is fully illustrated in his "small corner shop" cartoons with their myriad of products, tins, bottles, signs and such (May 7, 1985).

It is hoped that the reader gets as much enjoyment from looking through this collection as I had preparing it.

John Field

Police

During this period of continuing austerity, the black market prospered.

"Just a moment, Sir – pardon us if we seem a little inquisitive ..."

Daily Express, December 24, 1945

"I tell you I'm not a squatter – I've been to a sale and I live here."

Sunday Express, September 15, 1946

Following the end of the Second World War, the country suffered a long period of rationing of a wide range of commodities including petrol.

"Says they wouldn't let him have any 'E' coupons."

Daily Express, October 16, 1947

"Apart from saving the fare, I don't see a lot of sense in this Channel swimming craze."

Daily Express, July 26, 1949

"Gently, copper – lay even yer little finger on me and I could probably get yer a month for assault."

Daily Express, October 31, 1952

A State of Emergency was declared due to a 17-day National rail strike
which finished a few days after the appearance of this cartoon.

"If it ain't Bert Higgins! And us thinking he be up in Lunnun on strike duty."

Sunday Express, June 12, 1955

16

"I read this week that someone had himself stretched half an inch by an osteopath
to make him tall enough to join the Police Force, but don't ask me why."

Sunday Express, September 25, 1960

"Since they've heard about our pay increase this is the third time I've been slugged and had me wallet whipped."

Sunday Express, November 27, 1960

"Now let's get this straight – you say he flicked a spoonful of hot chop suey at you
so you flicked a spoonful of hot curry at him?"

Daily Express, November 22, 1962

Over 5,000 police were on duty, when King Paul and Queen Frederika of Greece arrived for a state visit in London, due to violent demonstrations on behalf of political prisoners in Greece.

"Nice work, lads – ninety-four demonstrators, one King, H.R.H., three bus conductors..."

Daily Express, July 11, 1963

"I'm not dead – but I've got a ticket and I'll be killed in the rush if the others find out."

Daily Express, October 29, 1963

"Do you know what I think is wrong with those figures, Copper?
They should be the other way round, that's what I think."

Sunday Express, January 24, 1965

"Sergeant doesn't think he received this lump upon the back of his head from a Chinese diplomat. He thinks he received it during the skirmish from your baton for cancelling your leave."

Daily Express, August 31, 1967

"Now which one stole your pocket money, sonny?"

Sunday Express, December 24, 1967

The day before this cartoon appeared, newspapers reported that gypsies were defying a parking ban at Epsom race course.

"We have a joker. Asked him his address and he says Tattenham Corner for this week."

Daily Express, June 3, 1969

"We assume you are not conversant with the rules of city motoring, Sir."

Daily Express, April 18, 1972

This cartoon appeared during a period of high IRA activities.

"Psst! If I informed you of the whereabouts of a £1 million IRA arms dump, do you think we could let your [sic] criminal charge of parking for ten minutes drop?"

Daily Express, August 9, 1973

"Music hath charms, Charlie boy"

Daily Express, October 23, 1973

"That's the bail for your son, Madam, now what about the bail for your husband?"

Daily Express, April 22, 1975

There was considerable animated debate taking place at this time about the relative seniority of vicars and church organists on certain aspects of the life of the church.

"'Come in Quasimodo' doesn't help, Vicar."

Daily Express, February 2, 1977

"The man says he don't believe I am your mummy, Ronnie."

Daily Express, September 21, 1977

"Great for our public image – the nick bunged full of drunk and disorderly birthday revellers."

Sunday Express, September 30, 1979

It had been reported that, at a league match, a policeman had marched onto the field, during play, to complain that a defender had sworn and that it was clearly audible to the crowd. The referee ignored his complaint and threatened to report him to the Football Association for interference.

"Remember men – any bad language from any of them, no charging on to the green."

Daily Express, September 25, 1980

"Here comes one of 'em without a seatbelt – cover me, I'm going in."

Sunday Express, January 30, 1983

"The new anti kerb-crawling Bill does not apply to us, Sir!"

Sunday Express, May 19, 1985

"Apart from trading without a licence to sell – I'm checking if bathwater can be sold on Sundays."

Sunday Express, November 10, 1985

"I only said, 'You wouldn't happen to be one of those Kissogram cops?'"

Daily Express, November 26, 1985

"Well, in view of everyone complaining about arming the police with fast machine guns..."

Sunday Express, January 12, 1986

"I'm jotting down a list of all the ones who aren't laughing their heads off."

Daily Express, February 17, 1987

This cartoon relates back to when weather forecaster, Michael Fish (first down the steps), got it badly wrong when he famously failed to warn television viewers about the disastrous October, 1987 gales. On this occasion the weathermen failed to give advance notice of Mediterranean-style sunshine with temperatures pushed up to the 60's. They had, in fact, forecast "showers and prolonged rain in all areas over the weekend."

"If you're coming to us for protection every time you get your weather forecast wrong you might as well move in."

Daily Express, March 28, 1989

Sport

The new Maracana Stadium in Rio de Janeiro opened that summer to host the FIFA World Cup. The Brazilian press called it "the biggest and best stadium in the world" and it attracted a great deal of admiration from the whole football world.

"Anybody got any ideas about running off to Rio half-way through the season?"

Sunday Express, August 20, 1950

In the Fifth Test at the Oval, a bouncer from Australia's fast bowler nearly knocked the cap off England's Len Hutton onto the wickets.

"Knock 'is 'at off – like Lindwall did 'Utton's".

Daily Express, August 18, 1953

A replica of the Mayflower arrived at Plymouth Harbor, USA, after 55 days at sea crossing the Atlantic.

"I see they had to tow it in."

Daily Express, June 14, 1957

"Can't you keep your confounded women out of sight?"

Daily Express, March 25, 1958

"The MCC sacking Wardle for saying rude things is one thing – sacking the Vicar for calling us
a bunch of incompetent silly mid-ons in his Parish Magazine is another."

Daily Express, August 21, 1958

This cartoon shows Raymond Glendenning, a very popular sports commentator at the time, who was equally at home with reporting on both boxing and horse racing. His distinctive broadcasting delivery was fast-flowing and very excitable.

" 'As they come into the straight, number one leads with a terrific right to the head – number two follows with a smart crack across the knuckles with his whip – another blow to the head – now it's number three who's in trouble! Number five's coming up with a beautiful right cross to the ear of number six – HE'S DOWN! and it's number two taking the lead – laying into everybody with his whip – ONE! TWO! ONE! TWO! – only one furlong to go before the bell...' "

Daily Express, June 11, 1959

"Should be a good game."

Daily Express, January 17, 1961

At the same time as the Henley Regatta, the Wimbledon lawn tennis championship was coinciding with the England v Pakistan test match.

"And I say your damn Wimbledon is interfering with my Test Match."

Daily Express, July 5, 1962

"Sid, there's a bloke hollering something about we're on his mooring. What's a mooring, Sid?"

Sunday Express, August 5, 1962

"Football would sure have a problem if they had to do like cricket – sort out the Gentlemen and Players."

Daily Express, November 29, 1962

"Excuse me while I have a word with this Mod about transistor radios."

Sunday Express, May 17, 1964

Three days earlier, a gang at Dagenham Greyhound Stadium had 'baulked' the public resulting in a possible winnings payout to the gang of £10m. A meeting of leading bookmakers and betting shop proprietors in London unanimously decided to declare forecast betting on the race void.

"Relax, sonny – we're not going to fix your Tote – we're just looking the joint over with a view to purchase."

Daily Express, July 3, 1964

"She always was a poor loser."

Daily Express, June 3, 1965

At this time, football hooliganism was so rife that it was being publicly condemned by the President of the Football League.

"Rodney! We are not at Soccer."

Daily Express, March 25, 1969

"That headline 'Mr Heath wants a wife' started something, Sir – little women in sailors' hats ... hundreds of 'em."

Daily Express, September 9, 1969

"Just what we need with half our force down with flu and the other half at the Springbok game."

Sunday Express, January 4, 1970

"Out!"

Daily Express, June 23, 1970

"I distinctly saw a disbelieving frown when the Umpire ruled 'Not out'."

Sunday Express, May 2, 1971

Two days before this cartoon appeared, a hoax telephone caller threatened to blow up the Cunard liner, QE2, with a full complement of passengers and crew aboard, unless a massive ransom was paid.

"Mind if I check your gear for bombs – some of them in this Club'll do anything to win a race."

Sunday Express, May 21, 1972

Martha! Come back at once!"

Sunday Express, July 1, 1973

Battle Royal Ascot. Football techniques come to the sport of kings.

Daily Express, June 20, 1974

"When you have finished your splendid impersonation of Dennis Lillee..."

Sunday Express, June 22, 1975

"Three hundred and ninety-four for one, don't you think it's time we changed Dennis Lillee?"

Sunday Express, August 3, 1975

"We'll get past Cape Horn before we tell them we've entered for the Round the World Race."

"So I awarded you a free kick – but referees come under the new no-kissing law like everyone else. Git orf!"

Daily Express, January 15, 1976

"Right! After that it's Mars Bars for the lot of you."

Sunday Express, August 19, 1979

"This will cheer you up – the Scout gives the same odds for you being in the first ten as he gives Ken Livingstone being Home Secretary in a Thatcher Government."

Daily Express, May 31, 1983

" 'I am not prepared to sit all afternoon discussing the merits of bringing back hanging
for umpires and linesmen, Mr McEnroe.' "

Sunday Express, June 26, 1983

"Heaven knows our game could do with a streaker, but I'm not sure Vicar's good lady wife is quite streaker material."

Sunday Express, June 8, 1986

During their 1988 tour of England, the West Indies cricket team enjoyed great success and won the Test series, drawing the first game and winning the other four.

"I always thought young Cowdrey was such a nice boy – I wonder what he did to deserve such a punishment."

Journalism

"When you've finished basking in all this reflected glory – one of you boys can slip out and get the Editor's tea."

Daily Express, November 15, 1945

"You one of 'em, bud?"

Sunday Express, December 5, 1954

72

"Is that Chapman Pincher?"

Daily Express, January 28, 1955

The long and difficult period of public debate, with the nation bitterly divided, surrounding Princess Margaret's desire to marry divorced Group Captain Peter Townsend, was nearing its end when this cartoon appeared. Two weeks later, the Princess announced that she was abandoning her plans for the marriage.

"If ever I lay lands on that little – who said he saw 'em take this road ..."

Daily Express, October 18, 1955

The Sexual Offences Act, 1956, covering a wide range of offences, was hitting the headlines at a time when the World was being shaken by Colonel Gamal Abdel Nasser, who became the second President of Egypt in June of that year. He had announced the nationalisation of the Suez Canal in July and this lead to the Suez Crisis, which started one month after this cartoon appeared.

"This Nasser certainly piloted that Clean-up-the-vice campaign off the front page.

Daily Express, September 20, 1956

"On behalf of the 'orse trade we appreciated your piece about polo and Cowdray Park, Miss Perrick."

At the Chelsea Flower Show, three days earlier, Prince Phillip had roared with laughter when two press photographers, waiting to 'shoot' him, got soaked when a lawn sprayer suddenly started to work. It was reported that no-one confessed to having seen the Prince actually press the button which controlled the sprayer but it was noted that "he was the nearest".

"Psst! Keep that ------ thing out of his reach until we've got our pictures."

Daily Express, May 28, 1959

"Good picture, Harry – just as you were saying 'He's bluffing, he wouldn't dare!'"

Daily Express, August 4, 1960

That month, Lord Beaverbrook, owner of the *Express* newspaper, was heavily criticised for running a 'sustained vendetta' against the Royal family. Prince Phillip's rather outright views on the paper are included in the cartoon's caption.

" 'The Express is a bloody awful newspaper,' said the Duke. 'Ah, well,' said Lord B., as they trotted him off to the Tower, 'at least he takes it or he wouldn't know it was a bloody awful newspaper.' "

Daily Express, March 22, 1962

Three days before this cartoon appeared, the Government admitted that Kim Philby, a journalist at the *Observer* newspaper, was, in fact, the ' Third Man', connected with the traitors, Burgess and Maclean, and that he had been under surveillance by the security service but had escaped to the Soviet Union.

"Three more, Sir – highly recommended by the Foreign Office."

Daily Express, July 4, 1963

It is obvious that the reporter had just returned from covering the Olympic Games in Mexico City where there was some violence and political demonstrations and also from the Isle of Skorpios, where the former US First Lady Jacqueline Kennedy was marrying Aristotle Onassis, and where reporters were not welcome. He is now being sent to cover the anti-Vietnam War protest in London where violence was expected and, in fact, over 200 people were arrested (with 86 people injured) in clashes with the police.

"For you, Archie – the Editor wants you to cover the protest march on Sunday."

Daily Express, October 22, 1968

"I don't think we'll have much trouble from a certain lady journalist 'reporting the fashion scene'."

Daily Express, June 19, 1973

"I've passed your message to the Editor, Sir – and one from me for sending me on this story."

Daily Express, January 6, 1981

"Which of you told the Press Lady Diana is staying with us for the weekend?"

Sunday Express, January 18, 1981

Another dig at fellow journalist, Jean Rook.

"One of them could be Jean Rook, which could be troublesome."

Daily Express, November 18, 1986

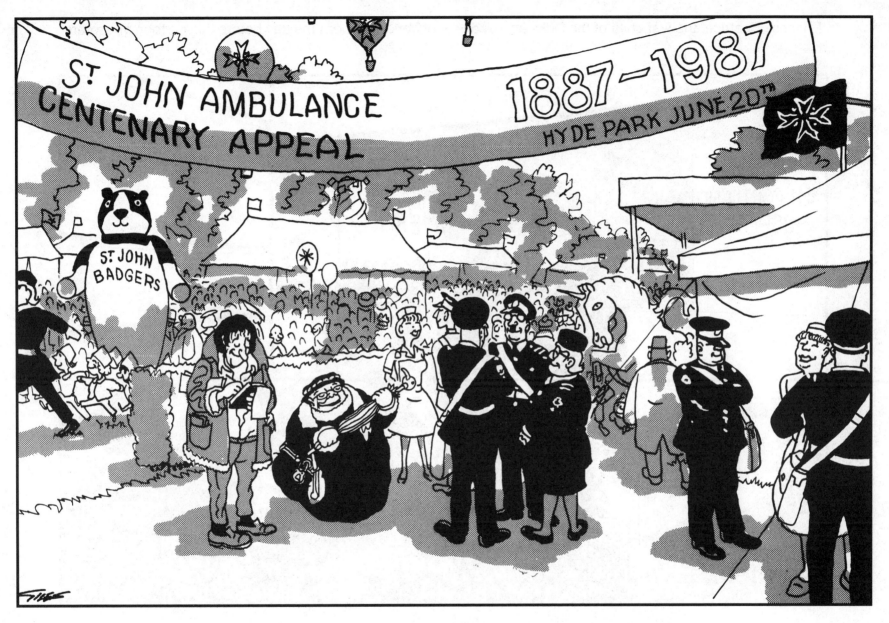

"You tell me once more you expect I was at their opening ceremony and you'll be needing them."

Sunday Express, June 21, 1987

Princess Beatrice, the first child of the Duke and Duchess of York, was born the day before this cartoon appeared.

"The Editor says he's not running 'The new fifth in line to the Throne looked like a stewed prune'."

Daily Express, August 9, 1988

"It's worth a couple of barrels off the head gillie to get a couple of shots of the Royal baby's smile."

Sunday Express, August 14, 1988

"I think it's their Jean Rook – I've never seen a Geisha Girl throw Zukiahso overhead in one."

Daily Express, February 23, 1989

"Unsociable lot, these Germans, sir."

Daily Express, October 5, 1944

"Nearly had to do without a cartoon in tomorrow's paper that time, didn't they?"

Daily Express, October 10, 1944

Night thoughts of a war correspondent sleeping in a Dutch hotel
which was previously occupied by the Germans.

Sunday Express, October 29, 1944

"Jolly dangerous, them blowing up these bridges like this, Sir."

Daily Express, November 1, 1944

"I'd sooner they sent us a few pullovers instead of cartoonists."

Daily Express, November 22, 1944

Giles in his studio in his home at Hillbrow Farm near Ipswich.

"Send up another lot of paper and rubbers – I'll get this smile somehow if I have to work all night."

Sunday Express, September 19, 1948

At Hillbrow Farm again with Joan, his wife,
trying to tidy up his studio.

95

"What's it going to be for today – Hydro-Bs or pigeon food?"

Daily Express, February 3, 1950

Giles had been ill for a few days and obviously the Giles family children
did not expect him to survive.

"Stop making holly wreaths, everybody – he's up."

Sunday Express, December 28, 1952

"He said 'Happy New Year' to everyone we met and when they'd gone a little way past he said 'and I hope you fall down a hole'."

Daily Express, January 1, 1953

Hold it, Mr Giles – that's not exactly what Mr. Williams meant.

Daily Express, March 31, 1964

[Programme cover for 1970 International *Daily Express* Powerboat Race]

Daily Express, August 22, 1970

The Economy

"Never mind where I got it from – they're not getting any increased fares out of me."

Sunday Express, June 2, 1946

Three days before this cartoon appeared the pound was devalued by 30%,
making a major impact on some food prices.

"Pardon my mirth."

Daily Express, September 21, 1949

"Upon learning of the coming price-increase on toys you did wilfully acquire these at a minimum price from your colleague, thinking they would be what you term 'big dough' come Christmas."

Daily Express, October 6, 1949

"It's no use pleading, honeybun. I warned you what would happen if the price of suits and shoes went up again."

Sunday Express, September 24, 1950

"I suppose if someone said elephants were going to be dearer we'd have a back-yard scheme for elephants."

Daily Express, September 26, 1950

"Now you've all decided it's cheaper to go by bus, I suppose I'll have to go by train."

Daily Express, February 27, 1951

"I bet she don't put me pension up."

Daily Express, April 6, 1951

"I see somebody's mother isn't prepared to pay the Board of Trade's extra sixpence in the pound for laundry."

Sunday Express, January 20, 1952

"Bloomin' shame – can't afford two bus fares now, so the poor little wife has to walk."

Sunday Express, March 2, 1952

"I see the price of ammunition's going up, Larry."

Daily Express, June 29, 1956

Severe flooding was being experienced in various parts of the country whilst, at the same time, central Government was debating the removal of rent control legislation.

"Boy, tell your mother it's the landlord called about the new rent increase."

Daily Express, February 19, 1957

Petrol rationing was in operation from the end of 1956 until May, 1957
due to shortages caused by the Suez Crisis.

"My husband was saying – by the number of times you go down to the sea on basic
he reckons you get 320 miles to the gallon."

Daily Express, March 5, 1957

"We'll have to lower their entrance price out of our tax relief – we're getting more 'Boos' than the ref ..."

Daily Express, April 11, 1957

"Morning, doctor."

Daily Express, September 10, 1957

Widespread drought in Britain and Western Europe limited butter production, causing frequent increases in price. The Government asked housewives not to buy unnecessary amounts of butter as this would further increase the price.

"If there's not a black market for butter in Little Puddleham how come everybody's ordering two hundredweight instead of their usual two ounces this week?"

Daily Express, November 12, 1959

"I can hear him – 'Make the most of this one, darling. After tomorrow you're buying your own.'"
– With apologies to the famous adv'ts.

Daily Express, June 6, 1961

"If you don't want to be put on dry bread and water
don't ask him what he's buying us for Christmas."

Daily Express, November 24, 1964

In a debate in the House of Lords regarding the establishment of Ombudsmen to investigate complaints of maladministration in Local Government, a spokesman for the Government said "By its very nature, Local Government is bound to provoke more complaints than central authorities" adding "we believe that Committee meetings should be open as of right as many Councils were too secretive".

"Very well, Madam. We promise to put your claim for a chain for your W.C. before the Chairman's claim for a £50,000 butterfly farm."

Daily Express, May 10, 1966

"Purely in the interest of power economy, Segovia – purely in the interest of power economy."

Sunday Express, September 3, 1967

"I shouldn't wear your new Tiara, Rosie. The natives are extra restless tonight."

Sunday Express, November 30, 1969

Two days before this cartoon appeared, meat prices were increased.

"Uncle Percy's little piece of beef cost 35p. Aunt Ivy's little piece of beef cost 35p..."

Sunday Express, June 4, 1972

"Don't you Merry Christmas me at 73p a gallon!"

Daily Express, December 19, 1974

"One day return Waterloo, please."

Standpipes were connected in various parts of the Country due to water shortages as local reservoirs reached their lowest levels in years.

"It don't take some of 'em long – 26p for the Scotch and 30p for the water."

Sunday Express, August 22, 1976

"If you really are going to put your head in the gas oven, darling, be a dear and do it before April 1st."

Daily Express, March 16, 1977

"I've been in and out of here for 60-odd years and I'm hanged if I can remember the last time
she told us her prices had gone down."

Daily Express, July, 12 1979

"Once it was: 'You've never had it so good,' now it's: 'You've had it worse,' tomorrow it'll probably be: 'You've had it!'"

Daily Express, March 25, 1980

"The wheels of the economy sure turn in a mysterious way – my 6% wage increase just pays his 9p a gallon increase."

Daily Express, March 11, 1982

"This explains why he brought me early morning tea – he's not going to pay the thieving moguls another 7p a gallon."

Sunday Express, August 17, 1986

"50p's worth of flowers and not too many orchids or red roses – his father used to make that joke with me 40 years ago."

Sunday Express, March 29, 1987

Shopping

"We've abominable robins, abominable Santa Clauses
at abominable prices – but no snowmen."

Daily Express, December 13, 1951

"The first thing you'll get if they enforce longer hours for shopworkers will be a slight fall in the standard of service."

Daily Express, November 20, 1952

"Perhaps your Editor would like to come and see the effect his 'Choose a Hat' competition
has had on certain elements of the public?"

Daily Express, March 2, 1953

"If Modom doesn't soon make her mind up, Modom is going to get a Yuletide ding across the back of the ear."

Daily Express, December 21, 1954

"Here comes somebody now. Ye gods – I hope THAT isn't mine."

Daily Express, April 3, 1958

"I don't care if they don't love him any more because he's engaged – that's the last lot of Tommy Steele we're buying today."

Sunday Express, June 15, 1958

"Lady says isn't it a pretty card but do we think the words suitable for her cousin Annie?"

Daily Express, December 15, 1959

"Yes, Modom, I did read that Lady Lewisham thinks some shopgirls 'hope their customers drop dead, preferably outside the store, before they have the bother of serving them', and I couldn't agree more."

Sunday Express, June 12, 1960

"If somebody doesn't stop whistling 'Little Donkey' somebody is going to get a little thick ear."

"Did you catch Miss Wintergreen's remark when I suggested her ensemble
was perhaps a little macabre for the first day of spring?"

Daily Express, March 21, 1961

"Miss! That was not the way to reply to Modom's request for a suggestion what to send her sister Millie."

Daily Express, December 14, 1961

Following the failure of a number of test flights, the Skybolt rocket was dropped from the Unites States' strategic weapons plans.

"Here comes another one – 'My-boy-says-Skybolts-are-out-of-date-can-he-change-it-for-a-Polaris?'"

Daily Express, December 13, 1962

"Ho, ho, another prodigal returns to the fold because the supermarts don't stock his favourite strong shag at cut price."

Daily Express, January 30, 1964

"Good heavens, no! I've just bought some extra woollies."

Daily Express, June 23, 1964

"Even if Modom was being a little difficult, telling her to go home and stuff her turkey is not in keeping with the festive customer-staff relationship of our store."

Daily Express, December 17, 1964

"You stay out of this!"

Daily Express, December 12, 1967

"How many times must I tell you not to accept I.O.U's."

Sunday Express, March 12, 1972

"We must shop earlier for Christmas next year Beatrix – I had to buy them the last thing they had left."

Sunday Express, November 14, 1976

"I assure you the fact that I haven't got a thing in the place to sell you has nothing to do with your husband being my bread supplier."

Sunday Express, December 18, 1977

At this time, there was concern about reports that some fruits, including oranges, had been injected with mercury by terrorists.

"I cut all me oranges open to show there's no mercury in 'em – now she's gorn and bought bleedin' apples!"

Daily Express, February 8, 1978

"He's first in the queue for the after-Christmas Sale. Sugar meece down half-price."

Daily Express, December 21, 1978

Six days before this cartoon appeared, Argentina had invaded the Falkland Islands.

"Here she comes – will we take back 200 tins of Argentine corned beef she's been hoarding since Suez?"

Daily Express, April 8, 1982

"I know she's not likely to carry many £50 notes – but with her we check the pounds."

"I can understand Joan Collins knocking five years off, but that one stuck ten years on to get her pension early."

Daily Express, September 6, 1984

"Lady! I've been reading doctor's handwriting all me life – your prescription says '24 Teddy Bears, I doz. horse pills and a box of mystique eyeshade'."

Daily Express, September 13, 1984

"Right! Bring her in – she's jumped the gun. Sunday trading doesn't start till 1986."

Sunday Express, November 25, 1984

This was the fortieth anniversary of the ending of the Second World War in Europe.

"I remember letting her have extra food rations for the Victory Street Party in 1945 – and we all know where they finished up."

Daily Express, May 7, 1985

"The benefits of Mrs. Thatcher's new Cabinet have not reached the public yet, Madam, embrocation and liver pills are the same price as yesterday."

Daily Express, September 5, 1985

Although Sunday opening of most shops was not permitted until the Sunday Trading Act, 1994, a number of smaller outlets, including corner and family-run shops were allowed to open. The debate at the time led to the formation of the Keep Sunday Special campaign.

"I bet he didn't buy those sugar meece because he likes them – he bought them because you don't get nicked for buying them on a Sunday."

Daily Express, December 3, 1989

"Sultanas, raisins, currants, 3 anti-tank missiles, 4 sub-machine guns, cinnamon, peel, brown sugar, 3 Challenger tanks, mixed spice, suet, 2 rocket firing sub-machines, nutmegs...."

Sunday Express, December 9, 1990

British Cartoon Archive

Carl Giles

All the cartoons in this book were copied from material in Carl Giles' own private archive, which is held by the British Cartoon Archive at the University of Kent.

The Giles archive was donated to the British Cartoon Archive in 2005, and contains a vast amount of material. It begins in 1942, the year before Giles joined the *Sunday Express*, because all his cartoons and papers from before that date were destroyed in the London Blitz. From that point onwards he kept almost everything, either at his farm at Witnesham or his studio in nearby Ipswich, and his private archive grew to include almost 6,000 original cartoon drawings and 1,500 cartoon prints, plus a vast image library of cuttings and photographs, correspondence, reference books, and studio paraphernalia.

As his artwork piled up, Giles wondered what to do with it. He joked that "I'll probably flog the lot!", but he only ever gave away his cartoon drawings to friends, or donated them to charity auctions. By his seventieth birthday he had so many drawings bundled up in his barn at Witnesham that he needed a strategy. "We could have a little fire one day," he said half-jokingly to one interviewer, "and solve the whole problem." But on his death in 1995 he in fact left his entire archive to a special Carl Giles Cartoon Trust, which donated it to the British Cartoon Archive ten years later.

The British Cartoon Archive has since catalogued the entire Giles archive, and made it freely available through its website at www.cartoons.ac.uk. Fans of Giles can now view nearly 8,500 of his cartoons from 1937 to 1993, plus almost 800 documents and photographs, from his wartime identity card – in his real name of Ronald Giles, which he hated – to pictures of his beloved yachts.

The British Cartoon Archive holds the national collection of political and social-comment cartoons from British newspapers and magazines. It has over 120,000 original drawings, and its catalogue at www.cartoons. ac.uk includes almost 160,000 cartoons, dating from 1790 to the present day.

Butch, Giles's Dog